101 reasons to have a

GLASS OF

WINE

AND A VAT LOAD OF

nonsense

Published in 2016 by Baker & Taylor UK Ltd
Bicester, Oxfordshire OX26 4ST

© Susanna Geoghegan Gift Publishing

Manuscript by Roffy
Contents layout: seagulls.net
Cover design: Milestone Creative

ISBN 978-1-910562-36-9

Printed in China

101 reasons to have a
GLASS OF
WINE
AND A VAT LOAD OF
Nonsense

This book is dedicated to Jay.

(With thanks to the case of
Anarkos Puglia Rosso 2012
consumed while writing it.)

WELCOME TO A WHOLE NEW LOOK AT THE WONDERFUL WORLD OF WINE!

We've all been there. It's the end of a hard day and you fancy a glass of your favourite tipple. But, as you reach for the corkscrew, a nagging voice – be it your conscience or your better half – asks, 'What are you doing that for?'

Well now the answer to that question is at hand. In fact, 101 answers.

Whatever your situation, one of these carefully crafted, scientifically proven reasons to have a glass of wine will prove the perfect retort.

Not only that, but you are holding three books in one. Alongside the reasons are 101 hand-picked wine facts. For example, in these pages you will discover:

– How many bubbles there are in
a bottle of Champagne
– Why a worm is your friend when
you want to open a bottle
– How long it would take you to drink
an acre of vineyard

And last and by no means least, we present the premier cru of wine related one-liners, proverbs, jokes and quotes from wine lovers throughout the ages. Right from the earliest philosophers to today's celebs – all offering their wit and wisdom in praise of the grape.

So pour yourself a glass of your favourite red, white or rosé, sit back and enjoy *101 Reasons To Have A Glass of Wine.*

CHEERS!

REASON #1

IT'S GOT MY NAME ON IT – CALL ME 'PINOT GRIGIO'.

WINE FACT

There are over 10,000 varieties of wine grape.

The best use of bad wine is to drive away poor relations.

FRENCH PROVERB

Wine ... the intellectual part of the meal.

ALEXANDRE DUMAS

REASON #2

THE RECIPE NEEDED A TEASPOON – THE REST WILL GO OFF.

WINE FACT

In his complete works, Henry Wadsworth Longfellow mentions wine over three hundred times.

Making good wine is a skill; making fine wine is an art.

ROBERT MONDAVI

Drink wine, and have the gout; drink none, and have the gout.

THOMAS COGAN

REASON #3

THIS WINE NEEDS 'OUT-OF-THE-BOX THINKING'.

WINE FACT

The wine box was pioneered in 1967 by Australian Thomas Angove.

A rich meal without wine is like an expensive automobile equipped with hard rubber tyres.

ROY LOUIS ALCIATORE

A cellar without wine, a home without woman, and a purse without money, are the three deadly plagues.

CYRUS REDDING

REASON #4

THE BROADBAND WON'T BE BACK ON FOR AN HOUR.

WINE FACT

In early 20th-century America, prohibitionists tried to prove that biblical celebrations of wine were for unfermented grape juice.

Boys shall not taste wine at all until they are eighteen years of age ... this is a precaution which has to be taken against the excitableness of youth.

PLATO

REASON #5

I RESCUED IT FROM THE 'BIN'.

WINE FACT

The highest vineyard in the world, Altura Maxima in Colome, Argentina, sits at an altitude of 10,206 feet (3,111 metres).

Wine is the blood of all France.

LOUIS BERTALL

After melon, wine is a felon.

FRENCH PROVERB

REASON #6

MY OLD MAN SAID FOLLOW THE VIN.

WINE FACT

After their breakup, Johnny Depp had his 'Winona Forever' tattoo altered to read 'Wino Forever'.

If a life of wine, women and song becomes too much, give up singing.

MARK SCHIESS

Wine prepares the heart for love, unless you take too much.

OVID

REASON #7

MY BODY IS A TEMPLE. I'VE DEDICATED IT TO DIONYSUS.

WINE FACT

Dionysus, the Greek God of Wine, was also known as 'The Betesticled'.

If white wine goes with fish, do white grapes go with sushi?

STEPHEN WRIGHT

Too much of anything is bad, but too much Champagne is just right.

MARK TWAIN

REASON #8

THE FATE OF THE WINE INDUSTRY DEPENDS ON ME.

WINE FACT

The first written mention of a corkscrew or 'bottlescrew' dates from 1681. It is described as 'a steel worm used for the drawing of corks out of bottles'.

That little sentence 'have the chill taken off' has done more harm than good than it is possible to imagine.

MARCEL BOULESTIN

REASON #9

I'M VERY
WELL RED.

WINE FACT

Britain owned Bordeaux for 300 years as it was part of the dowry when Eleanor of Aquitaine married Henry II.

Wine makes a man more pleased with himself; I do not say it makes him more pleasing to others.

SAMUEL JOHNSON

I drink Champagne when I win, to celebrate. And I drink Champagne when I lose, to console myself.

NAPOLEON BONAPARTE

REASON #10

I DO NOT NEED TO DRIVE OR OPERATE HEAVY MACHINERY.

WINE FACT

Tutankhamen's tomb contained wine jars labelled with the year, the name of the winemaker, and reviews such as 'very good wine'.

Either give me more wine or leave me alone.

RUMI, CIRCA 1200

Wine is sunlight held together by water.

GALILEO GALILEI

REASON #11

THE KIDS NEED THE CORK FOR A SCHOOL PROJECT.

WINE FACT

In Nigeria, a bride and groom are only considered married once they have shared a palm wine.

By wine we are generous made;
It furnishes fancy with wings;
Without it we should ne'er have had
Philosophers, poets or kings.

WINE AND WISDOM, 1710

REASON #12

NO ONE EVER GOT RSI FROM LIFTING A WINE GLASS.

WINE FACT

Madeira wine is heated to produce its distinctive taste. The technique was discovered by accident in the 15th century when fortified wines were baked in the heat of tropical voyages.

When wine sinks,
words swim.

SCOTTISH PROVERB

Religions change;
beer and wine remain.

HERVEY ALLEN

REASON #13

I SENSE A SEMILLON COMIN' ON.

WINE FACT

The Vikings called America 'Vinland' after the proliferation of grapevines they found there.

Wine is bottled poetry.

ROBERT LOUIS
STEVENSON

Wine is the glass
of the mind.

ERASMUS

REASON #14

EVERYTHING

LOOKS BETTER THROUGH ROSÉ TINTED GLASSES.

WINE FACT

Wine was not stored in glass bottles until the 17th century.

Never say the number, because it suggests that you are unable to pronounce the name of the wine you are ordering.

STEPHEN POTTER

It's a bold wine with a hint of sophistication and lacking in pretension. Actually, I was just talking about myself.

FROM THE FILM
FRENCH KISS

REASON #15

LASSIE TOLD ME THE WINE NEEDS RESCUING, IT'S TRAPPED IN THE BOTTLE.

WINE FACT

The pressure in a Champagne bottle is between 70 and 90 pounds per square inch, about the same as a tyre on a double-decker bus.

O thou invisible spirit of wine, if thou hast no name to be known by, let us call thee devil.

WILLIAM SHAKESPEARE

Wine has two defects: if you add water to it, you ruin it; if you do not add water to it, it ruins you.

SPANISH PROVERB

REASON #16

I BOUGHT THE BOTTLE FOR FUN, NOT FOR AN INVESTMENT.

WINE FACT

The vintage year for a wine is the year the grapes were picked.

It's true that red wine and fish don't mix.
I tried it and my Koi died.

REASON #17

THERE'S ROOM FOR ONE MORE BOTTLE IN THE RECYCLING BIN.

WINE FACT

Wine is stored in coloured bottles because it spoils when exposed to light.

What do you get if you drink German wine too fast? Hock-ups!

JULIAN CURRY

A pint of old Port and a devilled biscuit can hurt no man.

R.S. SURTEES

REASON #18

MY PALATE PREFERS A PROPER PINOT.

WINE FACT

Grapevines are rarely grown from seed. They are usually grown from grafts.

In water one sees one's own face;
But in wine one beholds the heart of another.

FRENCH PROVERB

REASON #19

YOU CAN'T SPELL 'WINE' WITHOUT 'WIN'.

WINE FACT

Trained pickers can pick
two tons of grapes a day.

Great is the fortune
of he who possesses
a good bottle, a good
book, a good friend.

MOLIÈRE

It takes a lot of
good beer to make
great wine.

**BRIAN O'DONNELL,
WINEMAKER**

REASON #20

MY SUPERPOWER IS MAKING WINE DISAPPEAR.

WINE FACT

Most cork comes from a type of oak tree called Quercus suber.

A meal without wine is called breakfast.

Advert for wine tasting event – 'Spit or swallow?'

REASON #21

I'M PRACTISING FOR A JOB AS CHIEF TASTER.

WINE FACT

Commandaria, a fortified dessert wine from Cyprus, is the oldest continuously produced wine; it dates back to 1000 BC.

Gentlemen, in the little moment that remains to us between the crisis and the catastrophe, we may as well drink a glass of Champagne.

PAUL CLAUDEL

REASON #22

'LET'S GO FOR A GLASS OF MILK AFTER WORK,' SAID NO ONE. EVER.

WINE FACT

In the James Bond films, our hero imbibes Champagne more than any other drink.

Wine in itself is an excellent thing.

POPE PIUS XII

The wine in the bottle does not quench thirst.

GEORGE HERBERT

REASON #23

IT'S NOT A WINE BOX, IT'S A CARDBOARDEAUX.

WINE FACT

The good people of Luxembourg drink the most wine per head in the world.

Champagne is the only drink that leaves a woman beautiful after drinking it.

MADAME DE POMPADOUR

What's the difference between a battery and a glass of wine?

A battery has a negative side.

REASON #24

A CUP OF TEA IS JUST NOT UP TO THE JOB.

WINE FACT

The 1993 Chateau Mouton-Rothschild label, a pencil drawing by French painter Balthus, was banned in the US for being pornographic.

Eat thy bread with joy, and drink thy wine with a merry heart.

ECCLESIASTES 9:10

I take baths because when I take a shower my wine gets watered down.

REASON #25

THIS GLASS OF WINE GOES GREAT WITH ANOTHER GLASS OF WINE.

WINE FACT

Bottles embossed with a crest have a notch in the bottom or side to help a labelling machine find the front.

Drink wine in winter for cold, and in summer for heat.

ENGLISH PROVERB

I'm only drinking white wine because I'm on a diet and I don't eat.

OLIVER REED

REASON #26

I'VE DRAWN A BLANC.

WINE FACT

The ancient Greeks considered it barbaric to drink wine straight – they always diluted it with at least 50% water.

Filmmaker and winemaker Francis Ford Coppola says, 'The two professions are almost the same. Each depends on source material and takes a lot of time to perfect. The big difference is that today's winemakers still worry about quality.'

REASON #27

ALONG WITH CHEESE AND CHOCOLATE, WINE'S A MAJOR FOOD GROUP.

WINE FACT

Italy has around 900,000 registered vineyards.

I only drink fortified wines during bad weather. Snowstorm, hurricane, tornado – I'm not particular, as long as it's bad. After all, any storm for a Port.

PAUL S. WINALSKI

There is more rubbish talked about wine and wine tasting than anything else. It is the perfect subject for the snob, the one-up man, the bore.

ANDRE LAUNAY

REASON #28

IT TAKES AGES TO GET A TAXI AROUND HERE.

WINE FACT

Portugal has a white wine grape called Borrado das Moscas. This translates as 'fly droppings'.

Drink wine, and you will sleep well. Sleep, and you will not sin. Avoid sin, and you will be saved. Ergo, drink wine and be saved.

MEDIEVAL GERMAN SAYING

REASON #29

I NEED TO BE SURE IT'S PERFECT BEFORE SHARING IT.

WINE FACT

Cork is harvested from trees that are at least 25 years old.

My dear girl, there are some things that just aren't done, such as drinking Dom Perignon '53 above the temperature of 38 degrees Fahrenheit. That's just as bad as listening to the Beatles without earmuffs!

FROM THE FILM *GOLDFINGER*

REASON #30

THIS ONE IS A SINGLE GRAPE - IT NEEDS SOME COMPANY.

WINE FACT

White Zinfandel and red Zinfandel are made from the same grape.

He has a hole under his nose that all his money runs into.

THOMAS FULLER

Penicillin cures, but wine makes people happy.

ALEXANDER FLEMING

REASON #31

I CAN RELATE TO SOMETHING COMPLEX AND FRUITY.

WINE FACT

Red wine drinkers are more likely to have a degree, be married and drink more frequently than those who prefer white or rosé.

As far as I am concerned there are two types of wine, those I like and those I don't.

ANDRÉ LAUNAY

Never drink bad wine out of compliment; self-preservation is the first law.

CHARLES TOVEY

REASON #32

CHAMPAGNE BUBBLES CONTAIN NO CALORIES.

WINE FACT

Englishman Dr Christopher Merret explained how to make sparkling wine in 1662, 35 years before Dom Perignon claimed to discover Champagne accidently.

One should always be drunk …
But with what? With wine, with poetry,
or with virtue, as you choose. But get drunk.

CHARLES BAUDELAIRE, CIRCA 1850

REASON #33

I HAVE GRAPE EXPECTATIONS.

WINE FACT

One ton of grapes makes about 720 bottles of wine.

Wine comes in at the mouth
And love comes in at the eye;
That's all we shall know for truth
Before we grow old and die.
I lift the glass to my mouth,
I look at you, and I sigh.

WILLIAM BUTLER YEATS

REASON #34

I NEED ONE MORE GLASS TO FILL THE DISHWASHER.

WINE FACT

Sabrage is a fancy way of opening a wine bottle by decapitating it with a sabre.

Wine gives courage and makes men apt for passion.

OVID

A man will be eloquent if you give him good wine.

RALPH WALDO EMERSON

REASON #35

BECAUSE AN EMPTY GLASS IS A SAD GLASS.

WINE FACT

There are an estimated 250 million bubbles in a bottle of Champagne.

The wine urges me on, the bewitching wine, which sets even a wise man to singing and to laughing gently and rouses him up to dance and brings forth words which were better unspoken.

HOMER, *THE ODYSSEY*

REASON #36

IT NEEDS DRINKING BEFORE IT COLLECTS ITS PENSION.

WINE FACT

The world's oldest bottle of wine dates back to AD 325 and was found near the town of Speyer, Germany, inside a Roman sarcophagus.

Drink wine, not labels.

DR MAYNARD AMERINE

I think this wine has been drunk before.

REASON #37

I THINK MY CALENDAR SAYS IT'S WINESDAY.

WINE FACT

Wine sealed with a cork is best stored on its side to prevent the cork drying out.

Sorrow can be alleviated by good sleep, a bath and a glass of wine.

THOMAS AQUINAS

If God forbade drinking, would He have made wine so good?

CARDINAL RICHELIEU

REASON #38

I DON'T NEED A +1 FOR MY BEST FRIEND'S WEDDING, DO I?

WINE FACT

Airén is the most widely grown wine grape variety in the world.

May we suffer as much sorrow as drops of wine we are about to leave in our glasses!

RUSSIAN TOAST

I'm dreaming of a white Christmas. But if the white runs out, I'll drink the red.

REASON #39

THIS IS WHAT THEY MEAN BY AROMATHERAPY?

WINE FACT

'Aroma' is the primary smell, based on its varietal. 'Bouquet' is formed during the ageing process.

Who does not love wine, women and song, Remains a fool his whole life long.

JOHANN HEINRICH VOSS

The great evil of wine is that it first seizes the feet; it is a crafty wrestler.

TITUS MACCIUS, 190 BC

REASON #40

I COULD CARVE UP A CAVA.

WINE FACT

The Code of Hammurabi from 1800 BC set a punishment for fraudulent wine sellers of drowning in a river.

'I rather like bad wine,' said Mr Mountchesney, 'one gets so bored with good wine.'

BENJAMIN DISRAELI,
SYBIL

Wine can clear
The vapours of despair
And make us light
as air.

JOHN GAY,
THE BEGGAR'S OPERA

REASON #41

THE CORKSCREW WAS A PRESENT, IT'S RUDE NOT TO USE IT.

WINE FACT

The term 'corkscrew' was not coined until 1720.

I once knew a fellow who chose
To sip wine through the end of his nose.
He said that the pleasure
Was quite beyond measure,
And curled up the ends of his toes.

JOHN PICKERSGILL

REASON #42

A GLASS OR TWO A DAY CAN REDUCE MY RISK OF GIVING A DAMN.

WINE FACT

The Hungarian Tokaji Esszencia, one of the world's finest dessert wines, contains up to 85% residual sugar.

Wine is the flower in the buttonhole of civilisation!

WERUMENS BENNING

Compromises are for relationships, not wine.

SIR ROBERT SCOTT CAYWOOD

REASON #43

THE CONTENTS OF THE BOTTLE NEED 'DOWNSIZING'.

WINE FACT

If you notice a hint of vanilla in your wine, it is likely to have been made using newer oak barrels.

For a gourmet wine is not a drink but a condiment, provided that your host has chosen correctly.

EDOUARD DE POMIANE

I told my wife that a man is like a fine wine … they always get better with age. The next day, she locked me in the wine cellar.

REASON #44

THE DENTIST ONLY SAID I COULDN'T *EAT* FOR TWO HOURS.

WINE FACT

The only book of the Old Testament that doesn't mention wine directly or indirectly is the Book of Jonah.

The Germans are exceedingly fond of
Rhine wines; they are put up in tall, slender
bottles, and are considered a pleasant beverage.
One tells them from vinegar by the label.

MARK TWAIN

REASON #45

I'M IN PARIS, IT'S 8AM, WHAT ELSE CAN I DO?

WINE FACT

Anthropologists believe early humans discovered alcohol by observing the strange behaviour of animals who had eaten fermenting fruit.

I've trained my dog to bring me a glass of red wine. He's a Bordeaux collie.

Drinking wine is just a part of life, like eating food.

FRANCIS FORD COPPOLA

REASON #46

IT MIGHT MAKE UP FOR
THAT DESSERT.

WINE FACT

The earliest evidence of
wine production dates back
to 6000 BC in Georgia.

Champagne and orange
juice is a great drink.
The orange improves
the Champagne. The
Champagne definitely
improves the orange.

PRINCE PHILIP

Wine snobbery,
of course, is part
showmanship,
part sophistication,
part knowledge
and part bluff.

LEONARD BERNSTEIN

REASON #47

I ENJOY BEING ASKED FOR ID AT THE BAR.

WINE FACT

Hold a wine glass by the stem rather than the bowl to avoid heating the wine with the hand.

I love everything that's old: old friends, old times, old manners, old books, old wine.

OLIVER GOLDSMITH

[Wine is] the best utilisation of solar energy that we have found.

EMILE PEYNAUD

REASON #48

THE LABEL SAYS IT GOES WELL WITH CHICKEN AND MOTHERS-IN-LAW.

WINE FACT

Due to pasteurisation, wine very rarely turns to vinegar.

Sir Hercules Langreish, on being asked,
'Have you finished all that Port (three bottles)
without assistance?' answered, 'No, not quite;
I had the assistance of a bottle of Madeira.'

CHARLES TOVEY, *WIT, WISDOM AND MORALS
DISTILLED FROM BACCHUS*

REASON #49

IT'S WHAT'S-HER-NAME'S BIRTHDAY.

WINE FACT

Oenophobia is the fear of wine.

A vicar was driving around his parish when a policeman pulled him over for speeding. The policeman smelt alcohol on the vicar's breath and then saw an empty bottle on the floor of the car.

He said, 'Father, have you been drinking?'

'Only water,' replied the vicar.

The policeman asked, 'Then why can I smell wine?'

The vicar picked up the bottle, smelt it and said, 'Praise be! He's done it again!'

REASON #50

THEY SAID ON THE NEWS THAT IT'S GOOD FOR ME.

WINE FACT

Hippocrates recommended wine for cooling fevers, as a general antiseptic and to help convalescence.

I needed a large glass of Chardonnay and a larger dose of Cary Grant.

TRACY KIELY, *MURDER AT LONGBOURN*

Age is just a number. It's totally irrelevant unless, of course, you happen to be a bottle of wine.

JOAN COLLINS

REASON #51

I NEED AN AFTERNOON NAPA.

WINE FACT

Californian wine producers began labelling their wine by grape variety in the 1940s, but the practice did not take off until the 1970s.

Let us have wine and women, mirth and laughter,
Sermons and soda water the day after.

LORD BYRON

REASON #52

I NEED AT LEAST ONE GLASS BEFORE I CAN PRONOUNCE THE NAME ON THE LABEL.

WINE FACT

Sales of white wine are 2% higher than red in the UK.

Bring in the bottled lightning, a clean tumbler and a corkscrew.

**CHARLES DICKENS,
NICHOLAS NICKLEBY**

You know you're becoming an adult when on a hot day you can't choose between ice cream and white wine.

REASON #53

THE HOUSEWORK CAN WAIT – I'LL PUT OFF VISITORS UNTIL MARCH.

WINE FACT

There are 20 million acres of grapes planted worldwide.

Men are like wine – some turn to vinegar, but most improve with age.

POPE JOHN XXIII

A bottle of good wine, like a good act, shines ever in the retrospect.

ROBERT LOUIS STEVENSON

REASON #54

'UNA COPA DE VINO, POR FAVOR'

IS ALL THE SPANISH I KNOW.

WINE FACT

The most common reason people buy a particular wine is because they are attracted by the packaging.

I can certainly see that you know your wine.
Most of the guests who stay here wouldn't know
the difference between Bordeaux and Claret.

BASIL FAWLTY, FAWLTY TOWERS

REASON #55

I WAS CLEANING THE BOTTLE AND ACCIDENTALLY OPENED IT.

WINE FACT

A flattened, round German wine bottle is called a Bocksbeutel, meaning 'ram's scrotum'.

I cook with wine; sometimes I even add it to the food.

W.C. FIELDS

He that drinks not wine after salad, is in danger of being sick.

JOHN COTGRAVE

REASON #56

IF I DON'T DRINK IT, SOMEONE ELSE WILL.

WINE FACT

The Languedoc-Roussillon region of southern France produces more wine than the entire United States.

A man who was fond of wine was offered some grapes at dessert after dinner. 'Much obliged,' said he, pushing the plate aside, 'I am not accustomed to take my wine in pills.'

JEAN ANTHELME BRILLAT-SAVARIN

REASON #57

I'M ON HOLD, I'M SURE THEY'LL BE WITH ME 'SHORTLY'.

WINE FACT

The Wine Cellar and Tasting Room
of the Rio Suite in Las Vegas, Nevada
showcases some 10,000 bottles,
valued at more than $10 million.

I have enjoyed great health at a great age because
every day since I can remember I have consumed
a bottle of wine except when I have not felt well.
Then I have consumed two bottles.

A BISHOP OF SEVILLE

REASON #58

THE FIRST THING ON MY BUCKET LIST IS A BUCKET OF WINE.

WINE FACT

Egg whites, bull's blood and gelatine have all been used to remove suspended particles from wine before bottling.

Wine ... the Mozart of the mouth.

GERARD DEPARDIEU

Lords are lordliest in their wine.

JOHN MILTON

REASON #59

I'M HAVING A BAD HAIR DAY.

WINE FACT

French oak barrels come from trees whose average age is 170 years.

Behold the rain which descends from heaven upon our vineyards. There it enters the roots of the vines, to be changed into wine – a constant proof that God loves us, and loves to see us happy.

BENJAMIN FRANKLIN

REASON #60

I JUST GOT A TEXT THAT SAYS 'WE NEED TO TALK'.

WINE FACT

Grapes consist of 15 – 25% sugar, but after the fermentation process, wine has only 1 – 2.5% sugar.

The best way to learn about wine is the drinking.

ALEXIS LICHINE

What I like to drink most is wine that belongs to others.

DIOGENES

REASON #61

THE LABEL IS PEELING OFF THE BOTTLE, I WON'T KNOW WHAT'S IN IT.

WINE FACT

Labels were first attached to wine bottles in the early 1700s. However, it took more than 150 years to find the right glue to hold them in place.

My only regret in life is that I did not drink more Champagne.

JOHN MAYNARD KEYNES

When it came to writing about wine, I did what almost everyone does – faked it.

ART BUCHWALD

REASON #62

MY AUCTION FINISHES IN 30 SECONDS.

WINE FACT

More people visit California's Napa Valley per year than Disneyland.

I drink it when I am happy, and when I am sad. I drink it when I am alone, and I find it indispensable for any social gathering. Otherwise I never touch it, except when I am thirsty.

LILIANE BOLLINGER

REASON #63

MY DANCING SKILLS WILL IMPROVE NO END.

WINE FACT

Women absorb about 30% more alcohol than men as they have less dehydrogenase, the enzyme that breaks down alcohol.

If the soup had been as warm as the wine, if the wine had been as old as the turkey, if the turkey had had a breast like the maid, it would have been a swell dinner.

DUNCAN HINES

As a rule, the Swiss, as wine-growers, must be admired more for the industry and perseverance they have shown than for any great result they have attained.

EDWARD L. BECKWITH

REASON #64

I NEED MORE ROOM IN THE FRIDGE.

WINE FACT

In 2015 the United States approved powdered wine for sale. A number of individual states moved to ban it within days.

An old man was seriously ill and wasn't expected to last the night. His wife asked if there was anything she could do to make him comfortable. He thought for a moment and then whispered, 'Perhaps a glass of vintage Port?'

She looked at him sternly and said, 'Now then, you know that's for the wake.'

REASON #65

I'M SURE I WAS A CORK IN A PREVIOUS LIFE.

WINE FACT

1cm³ of cork contains more than 40 million, fourteen-sided cells.

The English have a miraculous power of turning wine into water.

OSCAR WILDE

If the boffins are right and drinking a glass of red wine extends your life by a day, I'm going to live forever.

REASON #66

I'M OFF OUT ON THE
SHIRAZZLE.

WINE FACT

Up to 85% of a vine's flowers die without setting, never becoming grapes.

There comes a time in every woman's life when the only thing that helps is a glass of Champagne.

BETTE DAVIS

Ah! Bouteille mon amie, pourquoi vous videz-vous? (Ah! Bottle my friend, why do you empty yourself?)

MOLIÈRE

REASON #67

THE BOTTLE DOESN'T MENTION CALORIES SO I ASSUME THERE ARE NONE.

WINE FACT

A typical wine contains 86% water, 11.2% alcohol and 2.8% 'other'. The 'other' consists of around 250 compounds.

The juice of the grape is given to him that will use it wisely.

SIR WALTER SCOTT

I only drink Champagne when in love and when not.

CHRISTIAN POL ROGER

REASON #68

THAT SUPERMARKET TROLLEY HAD IT IN FOR ME FROM THE START.

WINE FACT

Portugal produces over half of the world's cork supply.

The people of the Mediterranean began to emerge from barbarism when they learnt to cultivate the olive and the vine.

THUCYDIDES

The juice of the grape is the liquid quintessence of concentrated sunbeams.

THOMAS LOVE PEACOCK

REASON #69

IT'S TOO LATE FOR COFFEE, TOO EARLY FOR BED.

WINE FACT

The wine lost to evaporation during ageing in oak barrels is known as 'La Part des Anges', or the 'Angels' Share'.

As a wine drinker, but not a wine expert, one's tastes are constantly changing.

ELIZABETH DAVID

Lord, give me coffee to change the things I can change, and wine to accept the things I can't.

REASON #70

I'M CELEBRATING
THAT I HAVE SOME WINE.

WINE FACT

Romans often preserved their wine by floating a thin layer of olive oil on top of it.

A man may surely take a glass of wine by his own fireside.

RICHARD BRINSLEY SHERIDAN, WHILE WATCHING HIS DRURY LANE THEATRE BURN DOWN

Excellent wine generates enthusiasm. And whatever you do with enthusiasm is generally successful.

PHILIPPE DE ROTHSCHILD

REASON #71

THIS HAPPY HOUR DESERVES TO BE A HAPPY EVENING.

WINE FACT

Grapes used for ice wine are harvested in mid-December at around 3 o'clock in the morning.

And Noah began to be an husbandman, and he planted a vineyard: And he drank of the wine, and was drunken; and he was uncovered within his tent.

GENESIS 9:20–21

REASON #72

I CAN'T AFFORD TO BUILD A CELLAR.

WINE FACT

When the Russian Bolsheviks stormed the Winter Palace in 1917, their revolution paused for a few days after they found the wine cellars.

Truth comes out in wine.

PLINY THE ELDER

Wine is the best liquor to wash glasses in.

JONATHAN SWIFT

REASON #73

IT'S MORE EFFICIENT THAN A RELAXATION CD.

WINE FACT

The first known reference to wine vintage comes from Pliny the Elder, who wrote that wine from 121 BC was 'of the highest excellence'.

Bad wine does me no harm. Because it never gets past my nose.

GEORGE SANDEMAN

Up to the age of forty eating is beneficial. After forty, drinking.

THE TALMUD, 200 BC

REASON #74

IT'S RED WINE

WITH BEEF. OR FISH. OR SALAD. OR MONDAY.

WINE FACT

Toasting dates back to the 16th century when a piece of toast was dropped into wine in the hope it would remove excessive acidity.

Wine cheers the sad, revives the old, inspires the young, makes weariness forget his toil.

LORD BYRON

I drink one glass for health, a second for refreshment, a third for a friend; but he that offers a fourth is an enemy.

SIR WILLIAM TEMPLE

REASON #75

I COULD MURDER A MERLOT.

WINE FACT

In 1825, after 200 years, winemakers abandoned glass stoppers.

Champagne has the taste of an apple peeled with a steel knife.

ALDOUS HUXLEY

If food is the body of good living, wine is its soul.

CLIFTON FADIMAN

REASON #76

IF I GOT THAT RAISE, I'D ONLY WASTE IT ON THINGS LIKE BILLS AND FOOD.

WINE FACT

The curly part of a corkscrew is called the worm.

Here's to a temperance supper
With water in glasses tall
And coffee and tea to end with
And me, not there at all!

ENGLISH TOAST

REASON #77

OTHERWISE THE GRAPES DIED FOR NOTHING.

WINE FACT

In the Middle Ages, wine from the Champagne region was flat and pale red. One called Bouzy Rouge is still made today.

Decanter: A vessel whose functions are most envied by the human stomach.

AMBROSE BIERCE

Wine is inspiring and adds greatly to the joy of living.

NAPOLEON BONAPARTE

REASON #78

IT'S PURELY MEDICINAL.

WINE FACT

Marilyn Monroe took a bath in 350 bottles of Champagne.

A retired woman was sipping on a glass of wine in the garden with her husband. 'I love you so much,' she said, 'I don't know how I could ever live without you.'

Her husband asked, 'Is that you or the wine talking?'

She replied, 'It's me … talking to the wine.'

REASON #79

HALF FULL OR HALF EMPTY, THERE'S STILL ROOM FOR MORE WINE.

WINE FACT

Kottabos was a game played by the ancient Greeks where players hurled their wine dregs at targets.

Beer is made by men, wine by God.

MARTIN LUTHER

Cheese, wine and a friend must be old to be good.

CUBAN PROVERB

REASON #80

IT CAN ONLY IMPROVE MY LETTER TO THE NEWSPAPER.

WINE FACT

Champagne literally means 'open country'.

At last I've seduced the au pair
On steak and a chocolate eclair,
Some peas and some chips,
Three Miracle Whips,
And a carafe of vin ordinaire.

CYRIL RAY

REASON #81

I SPOTTED AN EMPTY GLASS AND PHONED WINE, WINE, WINE.

WINE FACT

Feet are ideal for crushing grapes as they break them open, mash the skins and release the juice without grinding the seeds.

A barrel of wine can work more miracles than a church full of saints.

ITALIAN PROVERB

Drink a glass of wine after your soup and you steal a rouble from your doctor.

RUSSIAN PROVERB

REASON #82

IT WILL BE HOURS BEFORE IT'S SAFE
TO GO IN THE BATHROOM.

WINE FACT

There are at least a dozen patron saints of wine and winemaking.

Anyone who tries to make you believe that he knows all about wines is obviously a fake.

LEON ADAMS, *THE COMMONSENSE BOOK OF WINE*

Dinner at the Huntercombes' possessed only two dramatic features – the wine was a farce and the food a tragedy.

ANTHONY POWELL, *THE ACCEPTANCE WORLD*

REASON #83

MY STYLE IS CHABLIS CHIC.

WINE FACT

If you drank a bottle of wine a day, it would take eleven years to drink one acre of vineyard.

All wines should be tasted; some should only be sipped, but with others, drink the whole bottle.

PAULO COELHO

You appear to have emptied your wine cellar into your book seller.

THEODORE HOOK (TO A FRIEND DRINKING WITH THEIR PUBLISHER)

REASON #84

QUE SYRAH SYRAH.

WINE FACT

The Romans used lead to preserve and sweeten wine. Lead poisoning is said to be one reason behind the fall of Rome.

When you ask one friend to dine,
Give him your best wine!
When you ask two,
The second best will do!

HENRY WADSWORTH LONGFELLOW

REASON #85

A MILKSHAKE WOULD LOOK RIDICULOUS IN THIS CHAMPAGNE FLUTE.

WINE FACT

France produces over 300 million bottles of Champagne a year. The UK imports 31 million of them.

What's the difference between a pub and a wine bar?

About £3 a glass.

Go fetch to me a pint o' wine, an' fill it in a silver tassie.

ROBERT BURNS

REASON #86

I'VE JUST FOUND A MERLOT THAT PAIRS PERFECTLY WITH MY MOUTH.

WINE FACT

There are typically between 75 and 100 grapes in a glass of wine.

A census taker once tried to test me. I ate his liver with some fava beans and a nice Chianti.

FROM THE FILM *THE SILENCE OF THE LAMBS*

A man enters a store and says, '15 litres of wine please.'

'Did you bring a container for this?'

'You're speaking to it.'

REASON #87

THE GREAT THING ABOUT WINE IS EVERYTHING.

WINE FACT

In the UK, it was illegal to sell wine in bottles until the 1860s.

Quickly, bring me a beaker of wine, so that I may wet my mind and say something clever.

ARISTOPHANES

Champagne is appropriate for breakfast, lunch or dinner.

MADELINE PUCKETTE

REASON #88

I'M HAVING A WINE AND CHEESE PARTY. BY MYSELF. WITHOUT THE CHEESE.

WINE FACT

The colour in red wines comes from the grape skins.

It is well to remember that there are five reasons for drinking: the arrival of a friend; one's present or future thirst; the excellence of the wine; or any other reason.

LATIN PROVERB

This wine is too good for toast-drinking, my dear. You don't want to mix emotions up with a wine like that. You lose the taste.

ERNEST HEMINGWAY

REASON #89

I OPENED IT TO LET IT BREATHE, BUT IT NEEDS MOUTH-TO-MOUTH.

WINE FACT

Young wine used to cost more than old wine. Before the quality of bottles and corks improved, the older the wine, the more likely it had spoiled.

Good wine ruins the purse; bad wine ruins the stomach.

SPANISH PROVERB

This wine should be eaten, for it is much too good to be drunk.

JONATHAN SWIFT

REASON #90

I DON'T KNOW HOW TO GET THE CORK BACK IN THE BOTTLE.

WINE FACT

The largest bottle size for Champagne is called a Melchizedek, and is equal to 40 standard bottles.

Here's to the corkscrew – a useful key to unlock the storehouse of wit.

W.E.P. FRENCH

Conversation is the enemy of good wine and food.

ALFRED HITCHCOCK

REASON #91

IT'S WHAT THE INTERMISSION WAS DESIGNED FOR.

WINE FACT

Wine grapes are the single most widely planted fruit crop.

Champagne, if you are seeking the truth, is better than a lie detector.

GRAHAM GREENE

Wine is at the head of all medicines; where wine is lacking, drugs are necessary.

THE TALMUD, 200 BC

REASON #92

A NIGERIAN PRINCE HAS OFFERED ME A FORTUNE!

WINE FACT

A 'cork-tease' is someone who constantly talks about a great bottle of wine they own, but never opens it.

Is not wine the very essence of laughter?

MAURICE DES OMBIAUX

A waltz and a glass of wine invite an encore.

JOHANN STRAUSS

REASON #93

I'M DOING THIS PURELY FOR RESEARCH PURPOSES.

WINE FACT

Mexicans drink the least wine – less than a glass of wine per person per year.

Always carry a corkscrew and the wine shall provide itself.

BASIL BUNTING

Hide our ignorance as we will, an evening of wine soon reveals it.

HERACLITUS

REASON #94

EVERYTHING'S COMING UP ROSÉ.

WINE FACT

It takes four to five years from planting for a grape vine to become productive.

What did the grape say when the elephant stepped on him? Nothing, he just let out a little wine.

I used to have a mint vinyl copy of 'Red Red Wine' by UB40 until I spilt white wine on it and it disappeared.

REASON #95

THE DOCTOR SAID I NEEDED MORE FRUIT.

WINE FACT

It is traditional for European wines to be named after their geographic location and non-European wines to be named after the grape variety.

Quid enim Venus ebria curat. (Venus will do anything when she's drunk.)

JUVENAL

Take care of good wine and good wine will take care of you.

CHARLES WALTER BERRY

REASON #96

IT'S A MONDAY*
IT'S A TUESDAY*
IT'S A WEDNESDAY*
IT'S A THURSDAY*
IT'S A FRIDAY*
IT'S A SATURDAY*
IT'S A SUNDAY*

*DELETE AS APPROPRIATE

WINE FACT

In Ancient Egypt (around 1300 BC), commoners drank beer and the upper class drank wine.

REASON #97

MY KARAOKE VIDEO HAS GONE VIRAL.

WINE FACT

The tune for the US National Anthem comes from a song praising wine.

Strategy is buying a bottle of fine wine when you take a lady out for dinner. Tactics is getting her to drink it.

FRANK MUIR

One of the disadvantages of wine is that it makes a man mistake words for thoughts.

SAMUEL JOHNSON

REASON #98

I NEED TO WORK OUT IF IT'S
RED WINE OR WHITE WINE
THAT GOES WITH BREAKFAST.

WINE FACT

When Mount Vesuvius erupted in 79 AD, the lava buried more than 200 wine bars.

For when the wine is in, the wit is out.

THOMAS BECON

Wine ever pays for its lodging.

GEORGE HERBERT

REASON #99

I GAVE HIM HIS CÔTE AND SHOWED HIM THE D'OR.

WINE FACT

The longest recorded flight of a Champagne cork is over 177 feet (54 meters).

We want the finest wines available to humanity. And we want them here, and we want them now!

FROM THE FILM *WITHNAIL AND I*

REASON #100

MY THERAPIST TOLD ME NOT TO KEEP THINGS BOTTLED UP.

WINE FACT

98% of all commercially produced wine in the world is consumed within one week of purchase.

The person you converse with after the third bottle is not the same man who first sat down at the table with you.

JOSEPH ADDISON

Wine can be considered with good reason as the most healthful and hygienic of all beverages.

LOUIS PASTEUR

REASON #101

LIFE IS A CABERNET OLD CHUM.

WINE FACT

Studies show that red wine has slightly more health benefits than white.

Love wine like a constant mistress; never abuse it, and you will find it brings no sorrows.

CYRUS REDDING

Here's Champagne to your real friends And real pain to your sham friends!

IRISH TOAST

APPENDIX 1
THE HISTORY OF WINE
A TIMELINE

6000 BC – The earliest-known wine production starts in Georgia

Something about Romans

Today – you picked up your favourite bottle from the supermarket

About 5 minutes' time – you'll be enjoying a glass

APPENDIX 2
WINE APPRECIATION
A BEGINNER'S GUIDE

Step 1: Select a bottle of wine

Step 2: Open the bottle

Step 3: Pour yourself a glass

Step 4: Take a sip

Step 5: Think to yourself 'Am I enjoying this?'

Step 6: If the answer to Step 5 is 'Yes',
congratulations! You are appreciating wine!

If the answer to Step 5 is 'No',
go back to Step 1 and try again.

Repeat until there is no wine left.

APPENDIX 3
PAIRING WINE
A SIMPLE GUIDE
TO WINE SELECTION

Fish	A rich or sparking white.
Chicken	A rich white or light red.
Beef	A medium or bold red.
Last Night's Takeaway	I doubt you care.
Jennifer Aniston Romcom	Whatever's on 2-for-1.
Tax Return	Anything that might cheer you up.
Mother	A small glass of something nice.
Mother-in-law	A large glass of anything. Now.
Wine	More wine.
Beer	No, wine.
Water	I SAID WINE!!!!

If you've got the stamina for another round, why not try...